Jungle Animals

Siân Smith

Raintree is an imprint of Capstone Global Library Limited, a company incorporated in England and Wales having its registered office at 7 Pilgrim Street, London, EC4V 6LB – Registered company number: 6695582

www.raintreepublishers.co.uk
myorders@raintreepublishers.co.uk

First published in hardback in 2014
Paperback edition first published in 2015

Edited by Sian Smith and Diyan Leake
Designed by Marcus Bell
Picture research by Tracy Cummins
Production by Helen McCreath
Originated by Capstone Global Library Ltd
Printed and bound in China

ISBN 978 1 406 28065 4 (hardback)
18 17 16 15 14
10 9 8 7 6 5 4 3 2 1

ISBN 978 1 406 28072 2 (paperback)
19 18 17 16 15
10 9 8 7 6 5 4 3 2 1

British Library Cataloguing in Publication Data
Smith, Sian.
Jungle animals. -- (Animal in their habitats)
A full catalogue record for this book is available from the British Library.

Acknowledgements
We would like to thank the following for permission to reproduce photographs: Alamy pp. 13, 22 (© Gerard Velthuizen); Getty Images pp. 12 (Chris Mellor), p. 15 (Auscape / UIG); Shutterstock pp. 4 (jakit17), 5 (Dudarev Mikhail), 7 (neelsky), 8 (Sekar B), 9 (Matej Hudovernik), 10 (apiguide), 11, 22 (Vilainecrevette), 14 (Dr. Morley Read), 16 (Linn Currie), 17 (Dobermarane), 18 (Aleksey Stemmer), 19 (paytai), 21 (Matej Hudovernik), 20a (Terence), 20b (Seleznev Oleg), 20c (l i g h t p o e t), 20d (Johan Larson); Superstock p. 6 (Corbis).

Cover photograph of a Splendid Leaf frog (*Agalychnis calcarifer*) in Costa Rica reproduced with permission of Superstock (Minden Pictures).

Back cover photograph reproduced with permission of Shutterstock (neelsky).

We would like to thank Michael Bright for his invaluable help in the preparation of this book.

Every effort has been made to contact copyright holders of material reproduced in this book. Any omissions will be rectified in subsequent printings if notice is given to the publisher.

Contents

Animals in the jungle 4
All about jungles 20
What am I? 21
Picture glossary 22
Index 22
Notes for teachers and parents . 23
Word coverage 24

Animals in the jungle

This bat lives in the jungle.

This macaw lives in the jungle.

This black panther lives in the jungle.

This tiger lives in the jungle.

This monkey lives in the jungle.

This orang-utan lives in the jungle.

This gibbon lives in the jungle.

This sloth lives in the jungle.

This crocodile lives in the jungle.

This hippo lives in the jungle.

This ant lives in the jungle.

This beetle lives in the jungle.

This spider lives in the jungle.

This butterfly lives in the jungle.

This tree frog lives in the jungle.

This tree snake lives in the jungle.

All about jungles

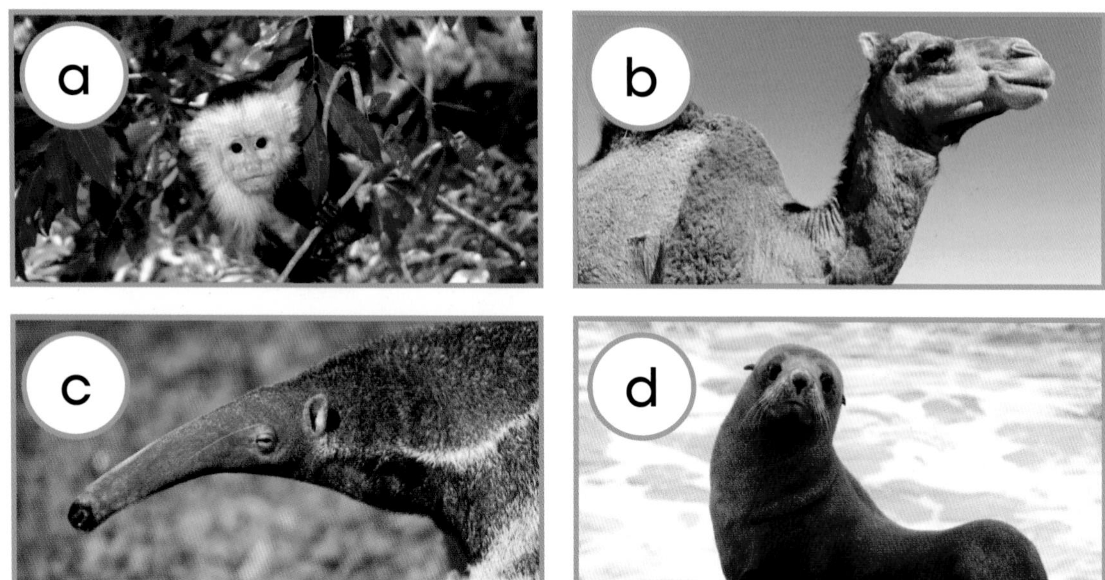

There are jungles all over the world.
A jungle has many trees. The weather in a jungle can be hot and wet.

Can you spot the animal that lives in a jungle?

Answer: a

What am I?

I have fingers and toes.

I have two long arms.

I like eating fruit and leaves.

I am orange and furry.

Answer: orang-utan

Picture glossary

gibbon

sloth

Index

bat 4

butterfly 17

crocodile 12

gibbon 10

hippo 13

orang-utan 9

sloth 11

tiger 7

Notes for teachers and parents

Before reading

Tuning in: Talk about why lots of animals live in jungles. Why might it be a good place for them to live?

After reading

Recall and reflection: Which jungle animals are in the trees? (bat, macaw, black panther, monkey, orang-utan, gibbon, sloth, butterfly, tree frog, tree snake) Which eight-legged animal lives in the rainforest? (spider)

Sentence knowledge: Help the child to count the number of words in each sentence.

Word knowledge (phonics): Encourage the child to point at the word *in* on any page. Sound out the phonemes in the word: *i-n*. Ask the child to sound out each letter as they point at it and then blend the sounds together to make the word *in*.

Word recognition: Challenge the child to race you to point at the word *lives* on any page.

Rounding off

Play the following quiz:

What might we see if we hear a:

whooping ... (gibbon)

screeching ... (macaw)

growling ... (black panther or tiger)

slithering ... (snake)

... noise?

In this book

Topic words
ant
bat
beetle
black panther
butterfly
crocodile
gibbon
hippo
jungle
macaw
monkey
orang-utan
sloth
spider
tiger
tree frog
tree snake

High-frequency words
in
the
this

Sentence stem
This _____ lives in the jungle.

Ask children to read these words:

bat	p. 4
black	p. 6
ant	p. 14
tree frog	p. 18